The Romance of Travel

The Romance of Travel

RONALD PEARSALL

TODTRI

This book was designed and produced by TODTRI Book Publishers
P.O. Box 572, New York, NY 10116-0572
Fax: (212) 695-6984
e-mail: todtri@mindspring.com

Printed and bound in Singapore

ISBN 1-57717-156-X

Visit us on the web!
www.todtri.com

Author: Ronald Pearsall

Publisher: Robert M. Tod
Editor: Nicolas Wright
Art Directorr: Ron Pickless
Typesetting & DTP: Blanc Verso UK

CONTENTS

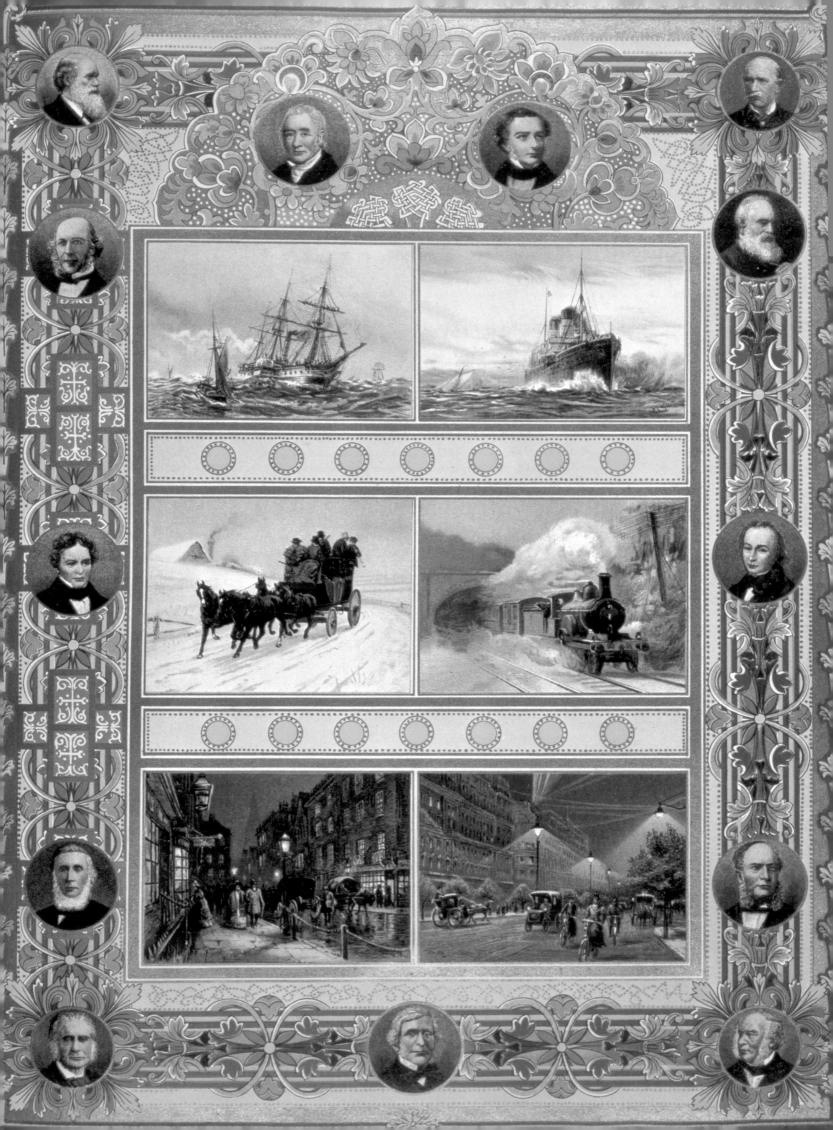

EARLY DAYS OF TRAVEL

Until less than 300 years ago travel for most people was something to be endured rather than enjoyed. There was precious little romance about it. Roads were muddy, dangerous, and the only form of transport was the horse. Goods were moved mainly by solid-wheeled wagons and a journey which today would take an hour or two could take days. Some goods also went by water and those countries, which had a network of rivers, such as Britain, were fortunate.

It was not always so. The Romans built a network of fine roads across Europe and Britain but when they were forced back to Italy by the barbarians these fell into disuse. There were roads of a kind, such as the Pilgrim's Way used by Christians on their way from Canterbury in England, but they were part of the penance. In the towns and cities things were better; roads were often

Above: In Chaucer's day travel was dangerous and difficult..

Opposite: The nineteenth century saw transport revolution, and this 1897 illustration sums it up perfectly with its "before and after" pictures

paid for by the travellers (tollbars date from 1267, tollgates or turnpikes from 1663). The standard of the road surface in, for example, London varied from street to street.

The ordinary people did not move about very much; some never left their villages. But with the coming of the Industrial Revolution in the eighteenth century something had to be done. A network of canals was built from 1759; in the end there was more canal mileage than navigable river mileage (2800 miles against 2500). Without the canal the Industrial Revolution would have taken longer to happen, though it is difficult to overestimate the enormous amount of cargo carried by river. What are now slumbering inland cities such as Worcester were major ports because the River Severn on which it stands – the longest river in England – was navigable for much of its length.

Slowly and surely road communications were improved. The highwaymen were subdued though they still hovered around the outskirts of London, but the risk of being captured by armed stage-coach passengers and the certainty of being hanged soon afterwards was a

deterrent. In the early nineteenth century Macadamising was introduced (granite and flint broken down into six ounce clippings), in one form or another still used today. Road surfaces were systematically improved. This was the great age of the stage coach, which had been introduced in the seventeenth century, and then was slow and hazardous. On long journeys horses were changed at coaching inns and travellers stretched their limbs or stayed overnight. The inns developed into hotels, especially in the towns and cities. The first hotel dates from 1764; *hotel* is the French word for a town house, and there was some doubt about what a hotel should be – certainly more of a house than an inn with its unsavoury connotations.

The stage coach undeniably represented a kind of romance of travel both in Britain, Europe, and later in America. But it was still slow by present day standards.

The rich travelled in their own carriages, and continued to do so well into the automobile age. The carriages were of various kinds – phaetons, landaus, barouches, broughams – and when the aristocracy did the Grand Tour of Europe, one of the requirements for a gentleman with Rome at the end of it, they and their servants went in convoy, often with great ceremony and in comparative luxury with every whim catered for so far as it was possible. They were a hardy lot, and often came back loaded with "antiquities", especially from Rome, though most, such as the Elgin Marbles now in the British Museum, were shipped back.

The railroad age made continental travel less exclusive. It opened up the west to the Americans. It was the beginning of a new chapter. Even the rich and the aristocracy could not buy the railroads off, though many tried, and refused to let the railroad through their land; they said that the trains would frighten their horses, demoralise the cattle, and bring madness and desolation to all. This, as we know, didn't happen. The railways came, slowly at first (the first locomotive built

Left: A stagecoach passing through a toll gate at night entitled Good night. This picture dates from 1835 and within a few years the stage coach would be obsolete, and with it the staging inns, many of which closed for ever.

Overleaf: The opening of the first public railway in the world, the English Stockton-Darlington railway in 1825. Few gave the new-fangled invention much of a chance of success, but far-seeing investors knew better, and were proved right.

9

Above: Horse-drawn carriages of the Saxon period, a lively but hopelessly inaccurate portrayal by the eighteenth-century antiquarian and historian Strutt. Travel was far less elegiac and the landscape far less picturesque.

by George Stephenson in 1814 travelled at 6 mph) but by 1825 the first passenger train was in operation. The first carriages were open-topped, but gradually they became more luxurious, culminating in Queen Victoria's Royal train which was more like a stately home on wheels. For the first time ever ordinary people could travel long distances on special excursions at giveaway prices; when they were given holidays and a half day off on Saturday they made the most of it. The railway was responsible for the seaside resort, Blackpool in England, Coney Island in the United States. There were exclusive railways for the better-off, the best-known being the Orient Express and the Pullman, palaces on wheels in which every whim was catered for. Few of the pioneers would have visualised the luxury of the classic trains.

Railway brought in the great hotels, often integrated with the railway stations. This was high living at its best and most ostentatious. Competition between hotels was intense, and to stay at the best, such as the Ritz or the Savoy, raised one in the social hierarchy. Food was as important as accommodation, and French chefs such as Escoffier were the new gods, bringing in haute cuisine. Eating, established in Victorian times as the main aim of life (ten courses were not unusual), became an art form.

More men and women now travelled for pleasure rather than necessity. In the age of the sailing ship sea travel had been uncomfortable and hazardous, always at the mercy of the elements. The steamship, at first a small utilitarian vessel without a future, flourished. They became floating hotels,

culminating in the *Titanic*, the *Mauretania* and the *Normandie*.

The same course was followed by aircraft; at first a thing of string and wires, within a few years it became an instrument of pleasurable travel, with the Empire flying boats, the short-lived Zeppelin, and the start of large-scale commercial flights by US pioneer aircraft such as the Douglas DC3 and the Boeing and in Europe by the Junkers JU 52.

Personalised travel proceeded at a great speed following the introduction of good roads. Strange-sounding vehicles such as landaus and cartouches drawn by a team of horses and often with an entourage of accompanying servants made their appearance, along with the bicycle, invented in 1866 and derived from the velocipede of 1818, pushed along by the feet like a chil-

dren's scooter. The first bicycle club was formed in London in 1875, the machines vying with horse-drawn vehicles, the carriages of the wealthy, and, eventually, the first motor-car. The motor-car was the vehicle of the well-to-do. Only with Henry Ford did it become available to almost all. The romance of travel for all had surely arrived. Rolls-Royce, Alfa-Romeo, Mercedes-Benz, Chevrolet and Delage produced their dream machines. And there was the motor-cycle, a young man's delight, and one of the most pleasurable means of transport if not the safest.

It was a golden age, without speed limits, traffic gridlocks and road rage, an age shattered by World War I, though within a few years the charm of travel was back on the agenda, this time for all without exception – the first tentative guided tours, the expedi-

Above: Arrival of Queen Victoria (1819 - 1901) at the railway station, Newcastle-upon-Tyne, in 1850, the magnificence of the station at odds with the still fairly primitive rolling stock. Queen Victoria used the railway frequently, making this form of transport extremely fashionable.

tions of everyday people in America to Europe, the first alarming crossing of the English Channel by Londoners who had never been further than Southend. Luxury coaches joined trains as a means of transport, the Jumbo jet enabled huge quantities of passengers to be off-loaded amongst bemused locals in far-off corners of the earth, motorists in increasingly more reliable cars drove hundreds of miles to explore areas hardly changed since the Middle Ages. Travel was no longer something special; it became commonplace, something to be taken for granted. Airports, such as Croydon near London, were no longer a few shacks but vast metropolises hosting duty-free shops and every facility known to mankind.

Is there still any romance in travel? For some there still is. And long may it be so as new innovations (trips to outer space perhaps?) appear, as they are bound to. To some, there is still a delight in cycling 20 miles to a beauty spot, or cantering a horse across the moors. In the final analysis, it is all in the mind.

Above: The French liner Normandie at Le Havre before its maiden voyage in 1935. Competition between the great nations for the lucrative trans-Atlantic route was at its peak, and for a time the Normandie had no rivals.

Left: Boarding an Imperial Airways airliner at Croydon, London in 1926, destination Paris, the most profitable short-haul route. The rich could fly to Paris for afternoon tea at Maxim's, but flying was still only for the privileged few.

BY RAIL

*A*lthough steam power had long been used, especially for pumping water from deep tin mines, the first passenger locomotive was invented by George Stephenson in 1815, named *Locomotion Number 1* travelling at six mph. By 1829 his son Robert's *The Rocket* achieved speeds of between 25 and 35 mph. It was not all plain sailing. Many thought that these great speeds would be too much for the passengers to cope with, and that they would even die, but there were sufficient entrepreneurs to back the Stephensons' projects.

The first railroad company in the world, the Stockton and Darlington railway in England, was opened in 1825. The Liverpool and Manchester railway was started in 1830. The occasion was notable for the death of the Member of Parliament, William Huskisson who was run over by one of the locomotives. Throughout the nine-

Above: At the opening of the Liverpool-Manchester Railway in England on September 15th 1830 six locomotives took part, but a shadow was cast over the proceedings by the death of the Member of Parliament William Huskisson, who was run over by one of the locomotives.

teenth century passenger casualties in Britain were heavy, sometimes as many as 1000 a year. This did not infringe the magic of rail travel, though for many passengers amongst the lower orders it was intensely uncomfortable; the first carriages were open-topped, and corridor trains were not introduced for many years; until quite recently corridor-less trains were frequently used on the shorter runs in the UK.

The early years were also marked by fraud and sharp practice, and one of those to profit was "the Railway King", George Hudson, who had inherited £30,000 in 1828, and recklessly invested. 1846 was known as the year of Railway Mania when 272 railway acts were passed, and panic seized the country as it was realised that the situation was getting out of control. A casualty was Hudson, who was accused of having cooked the accounts and paying dividends out of capital. He was found guilty, and lost his recently acquired fortune (though he continued to be a Member of Parliament until 1859!)

A government act of 1844 laid down that there would be cheap trains every day, so from the first it was a mode

Right: By 1929 when this poster was published, ordinary people had a choice of transport denied to previous generations. Railways, steamships and aircraft promoted their products vigorously, especially for the rapidly growing tourist. industry.

of transport that could be used by the mass of the people, the only mode of transport except the horse. It revolutionised life; with the granting of a half-day holiday on Saturday and easing of working conditions, trips to the seaside (and popular events such as public hangings where the railway companies laid on extra trains) were now common, and a host of seaside resorts such as Blackpool in England and Coney Island in the United States sprang up to cater for this new bewildered public, many of whom had never left their place of birth before.

The establishment of a railroad network in Britain was a colossal achievement. Tunnels were dug, viaducts were built, and great areas of towns and cities were razed to the ground to provide sites for the new great railway stations such as St Pancras in London. Some British cities sited their stations on the outskirts, such as Temple Meads in Bristol. For

first-class passengers travelling conditions were far removed from the upgraded cattle-trucks of the third-class, and what were known as the Pullman palace saloon cars were introduced in 1874 on the Midland railway in England and in America in 1863, and although these were not up to the luxurious standards of Queen Victoria's royal train (which was a miniature Buckingham Palace on wheels) no expense was spared to make rail travelling a memorable and pleasurable event. There was money in plenty, even if it meant ignoring safety regulations and paying railway employees starvation wages (in 1884 312,047 people were employed on the railways in the UK).

The coming of the train was the most important historical event of the nineteenth century, and without it the Industrial Revolution would have faltered. As important as the transportation of passengers was the

Above: The most famous train in the world and maybe the most romantic is the Orient Express from London to Constantinople (Istanbul in Turkey). No expense was spared, and every passenger's whim was catered for.

OverLeaf: An amusing artistic impression of an early nineteenth-century train. The coaches have obviously been converted from road coaches and those infortunate enough to sit on top, have been blackened by the smoke.

tions could be organised, and clocks needed to be absolutely accurate and set to a standard time (Greenwich Mean Time).All stations had their large clocks over the platforms, and this was emulated by the shops in towns and cities where large-face clocks jutted out above the sidewalks. The bible of the British railroad system was Bradshaw's, a huge book full of strictly adhered-to timetables.

The head start Britain had in rail was soon lost. In 1829 the United States purchased the British locomotive Stourbridge Lion, but it was not able to cope with uneven track and repeatedly overturned. The first US railroad was the Baltimore to Ohio line (Baltimore was then the second-largest city in the US). This line was extended to Wheeling in Virginia in 1852. The Americans were not happy with the gauge of British railways (four feet eight and a half inches) which they considered too narrow (as did the engineer I.K. Brunel who made the railway tracks wider when he built the Great Western Railway). It was also considered that the British train was grotesquely underpowered. The Stephensons had reckoned that a gradient of more than one per cent was impossible for a locomotive to cope with (thus the necessity for viaducts, tunnels, and a winding route), but the American disproved this and one of their locomotives managed a gradient of two point two per cent over 17 miles. The first US passenger-carrying locomotive was the Tom Thumb, built in 1830 for the Baltimore and Ohio Railroad.

In 1833 the longest railroad in the world

Above: George Stephenson (1781 - 1848)

Opposite: The great stations of London were monuments to British engineering and architectural

movement of freight; no longer would the canals and waterways be the main mode of transport. The train also stimulated inventions, such as the electric telegraph, so that the stationmasters could report on the progress of the trains to the next station, so that the signals could be activated. Time needed to be standardised so that rail connec-

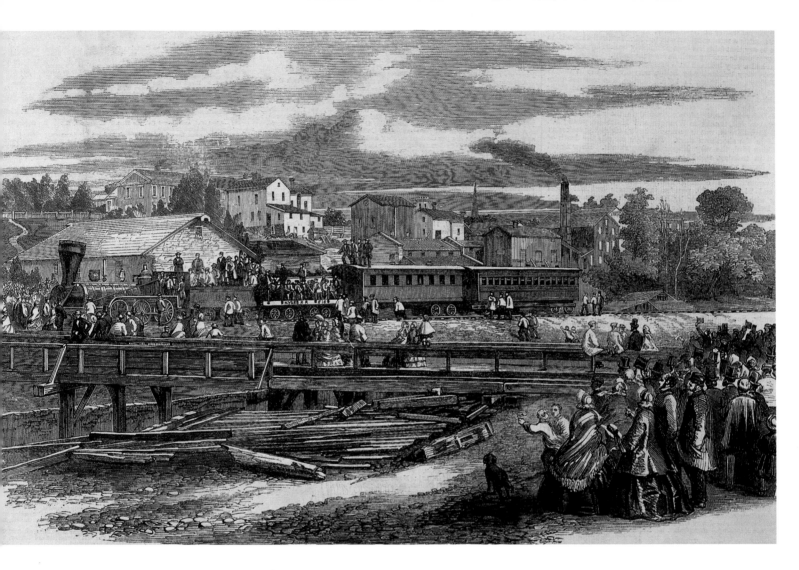

Above: The arrival of the first train of the Atlantic and Great Western railroad at Jamestown from New York in 1860. Even then American locomotives had the flared smoke-stacks that were to characterise the US train.

Previous pages: A pair of American express trains with flared smoke-stacks and cow-catchers, an enterprising invention when anything could be across the line as it went ever westwards.

was opened, the South Carolina Railroad, stretching 130 miles. This was mainly for the transport of cotton though passengers were occasionally carried as well. Frequently only one locomotive was necessary on this route. Railroad companies proliferated, with sharp practice common with surveys altered to suit the investors. By 1840 there were 3,328 miles of track in the United States, increasing ten-fold in the following 20 years. Initially cities and towns fairly close to each other were joined, but as locomotive technique improved the west was opened up and often the men laying the track were true pioneers, venturing into regions previously unknown. Typical of these adventurous railroad companies was the Southern Pacific Railroad of 1861, started by the four giants of railroad construction, Collis P. Huntington, Leland Stanford, Mark Hopkins, and Charles Crocker. It was con-

stantly being extended, and in 1877 a branch line from Southern California reached the Arizona border. Stops along the route for the taking on of fuel and water developed into towns, and the map of America was constantly transformed.

Many of these railroad companies merged in the 1880s to make new huge combines, and it was a sad day when the companies wound down their passenger services, some as recently as the 1970s.

In the UK the hundreds of companies began merging, and these super-companies gradually took on their own character and style which they zealously defended. Most had their own territories so there was often no direct competition, but they vied with each other to provide a fine service. In the UK the Great Western Railway became known in this century as God's Wonderful Railway after

the initial letters GWR because of its high standards; it was the first line to introduce corridor trains.

Because UK trains were relatively short-haul, passengers were aboard for only a limited amount of time, unlike in America where days and nights could be spent traversing the enormous distances. This was the true romance of travel, and it is easy to imagine the excitement of pioneers going west in search of a new life, transported at great speed and in safety and comfort. The dream was of a railroad which would cross the entire continent, and the Pacific Railroad Act of 1862 provided federal aid and loans. Two companies were concerned – the Central Pacific east from California and the Union Pacific west from Nebraska. The join-up was completed in 1869 at Promontory Point in Utah, near the great Salt Lake.

Trains in the United States took on their own distinctive look. Funnels of the locomotives were flared, and cowcatchers at the front of the engines were design features unknown in the UK. To an extent passengers were obliged to travel by railroad, but when in the early nineteenth century the motor car arrived the railroad companies were in direct competition for trade, and the trains became hotels on wheels, with lavish sleeping compartments, club cars, dining cars which provided cuisine comparable with the best French restaurants, and a rear open viewing platform, a marvellous feature oddly never taken up by the British train operators (probably because trains were often run in reverse on short trips). The trains were widely frequented by cardsharps and prostitutes. Businessmen, freed from the constraints of normal life, often succumbed and often arrived at their

Above: Cheap railroad rates for the less well-off had been built into railroad law in Britain, and excursions became popular even for those who had previously never left their home towns. The idea spread quickly to the United States, though whether people carried around so much luggage during the day, even in 1885, is open to doubt.

WILLS's CIGARETTES.

⑦   1ST LOCOMOTIVE IN THE U.S.A.

destinations fleeced of all their money and maybe carrying venereal disease. This was the underbelly of the railroad.

The romance which permeated rail travel can be gauged by the number of films with railway settings. *Union Station* (1950) with William Holden is set entirely in Grand Central Station, New York. The makers of the films knew that the audiences would empathise. Some were masterpieces, such as the British *Brief Encounter*, and the Tony Curtis – Jack Lemmon *Some Like It Hot*, and many had railway sequences at the heart of the action such as the classic *High Noon* and the Hitchcock triumph *The Thirty-Nine Steps*. Even more telling are the songs concerned with rail, nearly all of them from films. Who can forget *The Atchison, Topeka and the Santa Fe, Chattanooga Choo Choo, Toot, Toot, Tootsie, Goodbye, When the Midnight Choo-choo Leaves for Alabam*, and *Shuffle Off to Buffalo*? The back platforms of American trains have their own fans (*Twelve Angry Men* and *Double*

Indemnity). If there is romance about trains, there can't be much about automobiles! *Get Out and Get Under* of the 1920s is the only one to achieve any kind of status.

Trains featured in many of the early silent movie comedies such as Buster Keaton's *The General* and it is difficult to imagine a Mack Sennett comedy without a train slicing a car in two over level crossings. There was a love affair with the steam train, still on-going with all the steam railroad enthusiasts and a large number of privately run steam trains, epitomised by many children's books such as *Thomas the Tank Engine*, the model trains made by Hornby, and the British movie The *Titchfield Thunderbolt*, in which a venerable steam locomotive destined for the breaker's yard is brought back into service by a group of enthusiasts. This affection never fully spread to the diesel train (invented about 1920) or the electric train, invented in 1879, shown to great acclaim at an exhibition in Berlin in 1895, and later used on the

Above: The first locomotive in the United States as portrayed on a cigarette card. Whether it was the first locomotive built in the United States is not clear; the first used were English, rapidly discarded because they could not cope with the American tracks; the Americans preferred a wider gauge (as Brunel did with his Great Western Railway).

Opposite: Paris to London by rail and sea, though whether this was as popular as the other way, London to Paris, during the heyday of Paris is open to doubt.

Left: The Royal Train at Gosport in the Isle of Wight with Queen Victoria and Louis Philippe (1773 - 1850) in 1844 when he was King of France, four years before he was forced to abdicate and flee the country as "Mr Smith" by the Paris mob. The Royal Train was, even in these early days, a palace on wheels.

31

Baltimore and Ohio Railroad.

The railroad made mighty cities from modest towns. The first railroad from the east reached Chicago in 1852, and Chicago boomed as probably the biggest cattle-disembarking town in the world and as a great centre of rail communication. Between 1850 and 1860 Chicago's population grew from 29,000 to well over 100,000, and from 1885 six large railroad stations were built in the city to cope with the rail traffic.

This phenomenon happened throughout the world. In the UK Crewe and Swindon were virtually created by railways, Swindon because it made the trains, Crewe because it was at a vital conglomeration of tracks. Clapham Junction, an undistinguished inner suburb of London became the busiest junction in the UK.

The romance of trains can be matched by the romance of railroad stations which have been described as the cathedrals of the modern world. One of them, St Pancras in London, is modelled on a cathedral and mercifully survived a threat to demolish it in the 1960s. "Under the clock at Victoria Station" was a popular

Above: An advertisement for the Golden Arrow Pullman train from London to Paris, though the journey even as late as 1946 took eight and threequarters of an hour.

Left: Travelling First Class by Abraham Solomon, a good deal more comfortable than third class.

Overleaf: Travelling Third Class by the fine artist Abraham Solomon (1824 - 1862), painted about 1855, though by this time at least the passengers were not travelling in open carriages. Corridor trains were still well in the future.

rendezvous for lovers, and this famous clock is perhaps only matched by the clock in Grand Central Station in New York, a great station which has also been refurbished as a major work of architecture. Those who want to see Victorian railroad architecture at its best have only to go to Paddington Station in London and wonder at the great cast-iron and glass roof. The Euston arch in massive Greek style, a testimony to the railway age, was demolished in the systematic desecration of London that occurred in the 1950s and 1960s.

The stations of the steam-train era have a magical charm lost, alas, in the days of diesel and electric – the buffets with their ancient sandwiches under glass as if on exhibition, the mysterious liquid specified as tea, the innumerable platform machines dispensing chocolates and other eatables, the weighing machines, the coming and going of amiable porters, the loading and unloading of the mail

Above: Kellogg's improved sleeping car of 1877 for the US railroad. Such luxury was unknown in Britain and Europe where long-haul journeys were the exception rather than the rule and competition between railroad companies was languid.

Above: To many the El, the elevated railway of New York, was functional rather than romantic, but, as seen in this 1895 illustration, it was a great engineering achievement.

Previous pages: The departure, Gare D'Austerlitz, Paris by Paul Louis Delance 1848 - 1924.

carriages at immense speed, all gently enmeshed in the misty fog of steam. It was a time of happy greetings and sad departures, especially during the two world wars, but the railroad station of old has fixed itself in the nation's psyche. The stations of today are cleaner and more sanitized, so much so as to be depressing, and when a fine railroad station such as that in Birmingham, England, is demolished to make way for a concrete monstrosity it is time indeed to ponder the very question of progress.

The railroads produced their icons – the Flying Scotsman and The Mallard, a streamlined stylish train which perfectly reflected the 1930s, both dwarfed in size by Big Boy,

operating between 1941 and 1944 on the Union Pacific Railroad. It weighed 604 tons, and was 132 feet (40 metres) long. It was one of the last of the leviathans of the track in a country where the locomotives were usually huge anyway. After 1865 there was a general consensus as to the lay-out of the wheels – four driving wheels and four pilot wheels. These proved insufficient when steam technology allowed the creation of much larger locomotives. In the golden age of steam, American locomotives had 16 drive wheels, each seven feet in diameter; they could pull 20 carriages at 75 mph.

Certainly the most famous railroad in the world is the Orient Express that ran from

Paris to Constantinople (Istanbul) for more than 80 years (1883 – 1977). It was Europe's first transcontinental express, initially covering a route of more than 1700 miles (about 2740 km) including brief stopovers in cities such as Munich, Vienna, Budapest and Bucharest. During its first journeys the passengers disembarked at the Bulgarian port of Varna and ferried across the Black Sea to Constantinople, but in 1889 the entire trip was by rail. La Compagnie Internationale des Wagons-Lits et des Grands Express Européens furnished the train, which had lavish sleeping, restaurant and salon cars, smoking cars and ladies' drawing rooms. With its Oriental rugs, velvet upholstery, mahogany panelling, and deep leather armchairs the Orient Express was unmatched. The chefs provided the ultimate in high cuisine, and the Orient Express attracted the elite of society including royalty. The glamour of the train captivated many writers such as Graham Greene and Agatha Christie, whose Murder on the Orient Express was lavishly filmed with a close attention paid to authenticity. This was romantic travel at its pinnacle, but with the speed and convenience of air travel the languor, slow tempo, and sophistication of the Orient Express began to lose its appeal and in 1977 after several decades of declining patronage it was discontinued, though an American, James Sherwood, revived the concept in 1982 with the Venice Simplon Orient Express with several routes between London and Venice.

If the American long-distance train was a city on wheels the Trans-Siberian Railroad was a Russian village on wheels, with vast free-standing iron stoves and vendors on the platforms of the stations selling the passengers food. If any one railroad retains its mystery and spirit of adventure it is the Trans-Siberian. Conceived by Tsar Alexander III, the construction began in 1891, and as in America it proceeded from the west (Moscow) and the east (Vladivostok) by way of existing railroads such as the Mid-Siberian Railway.

The original aim was to build a line directly across Manchuria, and the builders obtained permission from the Chinese to do so. This was completed in 1904, but after the Russo-Japanese War of 1904-05 (which Japan conclusively won) the Russians wisely opted for a longer route, and this, despite World War I, was finished in 1916. This railroad marked a turning point in the history of Siberia, opening it up to commercial exploitation, an open-ended task as spur lines, including tracks through permafrost and swamps, continue to be built. The distance was 5778 miles (9198 km) between Moscow and Vladivostok, but the line stretched even further, to the port of Nakhodka, 5867 miles from Moscow. The full rail trip takes about eight days with an overnight stop in Khabarovsk. It was a mammoth achievement considering the inhospitable terrain, ranking with the American transcontinental line.

Romance does not necessarily involve long-haul trains. The El, the elevated railway in New York, has its devotees, and few Londoners can forget the luxurious Pullman car, the Brighton Belle, which made the 60 mile trip from London to Brighton the south coast, a delightful experience. And there was the Metropolitan Line from London used by commuters as little towns were built up along its route in the 1920s. This part of the country no more than half an hour from the centre of London was known as Metroland. Romance is where one finds it. Even the dirty "milk trains" of the industrial heartland of England running in the early hours of the morning for miners and shift workers had their passionate supporters.

In both the United States and the UK the user-friendly character of the railroad networks was skillfully promoted by clever poster and advertising campaigns. Many of the posters, by superb artists, have become collectors' items, even though at the time they were ephemera designed to sell a product – hassle-free travel. And during the great age of steam it was hassle free, a joy for all.

BY SEA

Above: Advert for the maiden voyage, issued by the Great Ship Company.

By the end of the eighteenth century small steamships were plying the rivers and inland waterways of the United States, Britain and France, but they were grossly underpowered and no future was seen in them in a sea-going role except as tugs in coastal waters. The first passenger steamship was the *Comet*, plying the River Clyde in Scotland in the early nineteenth century. They were all paddle steamers, usually with a paddle at each side of the hull, but the later most famous paddle steamers, the Mississippi steamers, had one wheel at the stern. All this was to change, due entirely to one man who was 50 years ahead of his time, Isambard Kingdom Brunel, who was thought to be mad when he decided to build an ocean-going steamship, the *Great Western*, though he took the precaution of having sails as well, as did all the early steamships.

Opposite: The Cruise by Fernand Toussaint (1873 - 1955), hardly a good advertisement as the passengers look extremely bored.

The credit for being the first sea-going steamship to go into *commercial* service goes to the ninety-ton *Rob Roy* of 1819 which plied between Scotland and Ireland, and it so impressed the French that they bought it for a cross-channel service between Dover and Calais. In 1809 a 150-mile run between Perth Ambrey, New Jersey and Delaware Bay showed the viability of ocean travel by steamships.

By the time Queen Victoria came to the British throne in 1837 "steam packets", as they were known, operated on a number of routes between Britain, Ireland, and the Continent. The first "steamship" to cross any ocean was the American *Savannah* in 1819, but she used steam power as an auxiliary to sail. In a voyage of 27 days from Savannah to Liverpool she steamed for only 85 hours.

The story of the epoch-making *Great Western* starts in 1835 when the railroad between London and Bristol was being built. Brunel suggested that the line could be "extended" to New York by using a steamship. Bristol merchants thought it worth trying and put up the money. The *Great Western* was built in the traditional manner of oak, though wood was soon replaced by iron

and later still by steel, and paddles soon gave way to the propeller or screw. Brunel had in mind a luxury vessel and no expense was spared in the fittings, but other contenders were entering the arena and the battle to cross the Atlantic first was narrowly won by a small converted steam packet, the *Sirius*, the captain of which had to burn part of his cargo as he was running short of fuel. The *Great Western* arrived soon after in New York, to massive acclaim; 236 feet long, 59.8 feet broad, nothing had been seen like it before. Transatlantic travel had begun. The *Great Western* did 67 crossings in eight years; not only was she the safest, but the fastest, her best crossing taking twelve days six hours.

Brunel did not rest on his laurels, and set to work on a larger ship, the *Great Britain,* with screw propulsion and an iron hull. Launched in 1843, it did four round trips to

New York, then ran into difficulties, and was beached in Northern Ireland. The master had used incorrect charts, and the iron hull had affected the compass. The *Great Britain* was in commission until 1886, then used as a storage hulk in the Falkland Islands until 1937 when she was beached. She was later brought back to display in Bristol, the first iron screw-propelled steamship in the world.

Brunel's third ship, the *Great Eastern*, dwarfed everything that had gone before. 692 feet long, with a displacement of 32,000 tons, it was intended for the Australia run round the Cape of Good Hope. It was the prototype of all later ocean liners – except that it was stronger; wrought iron does not rust like steel. Until the construction of the *Titanic* and her sister ship it was the longest ship in the world. In one accident when she struck a hidden uncharted reef in Long Island Sound and

Above: Brunel's Great Eastern in full steam and under full sail, with its characteristic five funnels and huge port and starboard paddle wheels.

Opposite: One of the greatest of the steamships, the Aquitania is less well known than its contemporaries as it enjoyed a long, profitable and trouble-free life.

Overleaf: A recreation by Harley Crossley of the Titanic departing from Southampton.

centration of power ever known (over 8000 i.h.p), but was still underpowered for its size and purpose. The launch in 1858 was fraught with difficulties, the maiden voyage was marred by a serious explosion, and Brunel died from an illness caused by stress. Commercially, the *Great Eastern* was not a success; in fact, it was disastrous. The Australian trade for which it had been built had slumped and by the time it had recovered the Suez Canal had been opened, and the ship was too big to pass through. It was kept to Transatlantic runs, but was too large for the demand; there were insufficient passengers which in retrospect is rather surprising as emigrants from Ireland, hit by the potato famine, ran into millions. Eventually she was used as a cable layer; in 1866 at a second attempt she laid the first successful Atlantic telegraph cable between Europe and the New World.

Other nations kept a close eye on the British shipbuilders, profiting from their skills and their inventiveness. When the steersman of the *Great Eastern* lost control over his two huge steering wheels in horrendous weather, steam steering wheels were invented, controlled by a miniature wheel on the bridge. There were still problems. Immense amounts of fuel had been needed. This often had to be transported from Wales to suitable coaling stations such as the Cape of Good

Above: Less known than his photograph in a "stovepipe" hat standing by one of his steamship's gigantic screws (propellers), this is a thoughtful portrait of Brunel at his desk.

a hole 85 feet long was torn in the outer plating none of the passengers was aware of anything amiss. She would no doubt have survived the iceberg collision that sank the Titanic.

She was so heavy that both screw and paddle were used. The propeller measured 25 feet across. The *Great Eastern* had the greatest con-

Hope for the long journey to Australia. By the 1860s most problems had been solved. Indeed, the ultimate fast sailing ship, the tea clipper, used steamship technology in its design.

Britain, so long the pioneer, was losing out in technology to the Germans and the Americans, and the first superliner, the *Kaiser Wilhelm der Grosse*, was launched in 1897. The liners were a critical factor in immigration to the New World and until 1921, when stricter laws came into being, New York alone accepted a million emigrants a year. They were packed into dormitories with hard bunks and basic amenities. Usually they provided their own food, and were kept well out of sight of the better-off. Some of them traversed the Atlantic for no more than $20, but the sheer numbers provided a core income for the shipping companies and enabled them to invest in ever more breathtaking ships, though those travelling third class or steerage hardly benefited. Hidden in the bowels of the ship, they were the most vulnerable should tragedy strike, and although the *Titanic* is the best-known example many other ships were lost too, often through negligence, greed on the part of the shipping lines who ignored safety requirements and communication problems.

Away from the busy Transatlantic route, the European empires sent their civil servants, soldiers, merchants and colonists all over the world, many of them travelling in the height of luxury. The commuting between Britain and India produced the word "posh", meaning superior, from the initial letters of the phrase "Port Out Starboard Home" as this was thought the most enjoyable side of the ship. There is no doubt that the shipping lines found the Atlantic run the most prestigious,

Above: An advertisement of 1898 for the Hamburg-American Line for their Orient routes with a symbolic crescent to represent the east.

and all nations vied for the Blue Riband, awarded to the vessels which were fastest across the Atlantic. It passed from country to country. The German *Bremen* held it for eight years; the British *Mauretania* for even longer, the Hamburg-America Line's *Deutschland* for six.

Rivalry between Germany and Britain was intense; after the success of the German superliners the British government subsidized the steam-turbine-driven *Lusitania* and *Mauretania*, which established new standards in luxury, speed, and comfort.

Voyages across the Atlantic were not just one way. America had become the richest nation in the world. Americans crossed to Britain and Europe in their thousands. Sometimes, such as the American novelist Henry James, they stayed. Many rich American women came to Britain to seek hus-

bands amongst the increasingly impoverished British aristocracy. There was also a stream of Americans to Britain and Ireland searching for their roots. Paris, the centre of the artistic world, was also a major attraction; James McNeill Whistler, the artist, born in Lowell, Massachusetts, took up residence in Paris in 1857 to study art. It proved a magnet right up to the start of World War II. For the American super-rich only the best was good enough, and they also looked for the modern, the up-to-date, something which reflected their attitudes and the steamship lines were only too happy to oblige.

Whereas the Europeans and the British were often content with faded elegance and were often frightened by the unfamiliar and novel, the Americans wanted unashamed luxury, en suite bedrooms in their staterooms and a variety of pursuits to wile away the

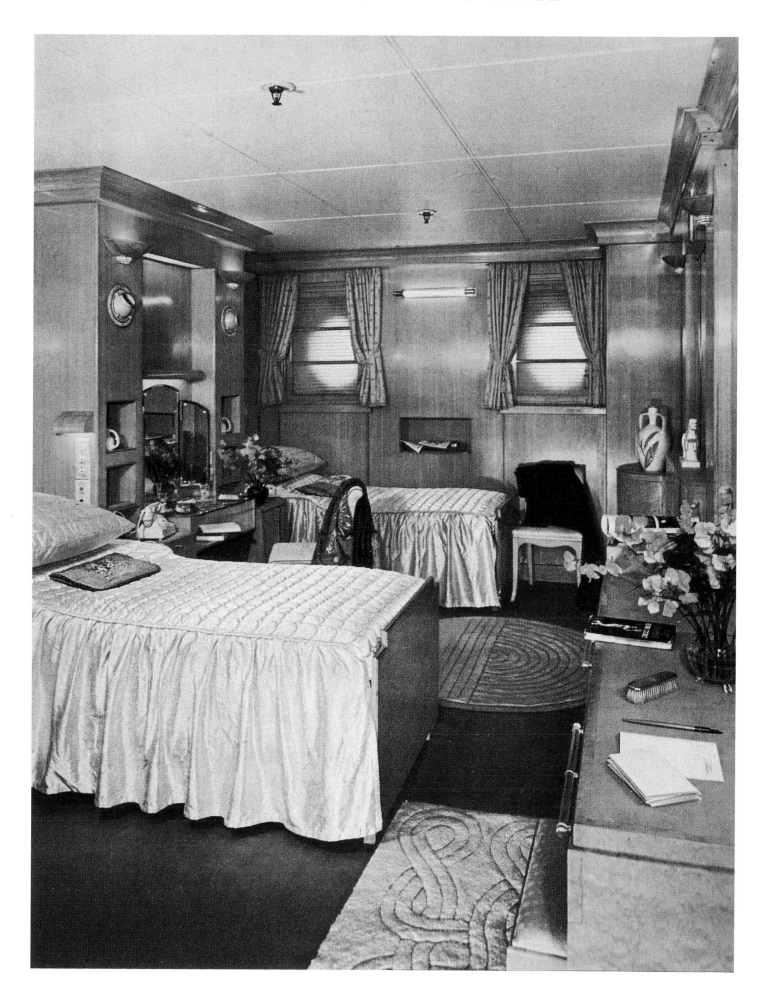

CUNARD LINE
LIVERPOOL
TO
NEW YORK & BOSTON

R.M.S "LUSITANIÄ"
FIRST CLASS
DINING SALOON

hours. The names of the ships were unashamedly boastful – the *Gigantic*, the *Olympic*, and the German *Imperator*, 919 feet long and weighing 52,117 tons. The interiors of the liners were not always governed by taste, and many of them were like monstrous hotels with sweeping staircases and lavish decor carried out in a variety of styles to suit the optimum consumer. Some liners were decorated in a manner that the shipping lines reckoned to be English aristocratic – heavy, plush and cluttered – and there are curiosities

Left: Cruise Ship of 1882, an evocative oil painting by George Wright, in which all the pleasurable elements of sea travel (including a shipboard romance) are conjured up

such as the art nouveau stylism of the first-class lounge of the *Kaiser Wilhem der Grosse* which clashes with the furniture which is contorted High Victorian. The effect is ponderous and oppressive.

For their *Cap Arcona*, destined for the Hamburg – South America run, the Germans created what they imagined was a South American theme, with masses of plants and exotic decor in the on-board winter garden, though the provision of wicker chairs is derived from the fashionable use of wicker

Right: The four-funnel Mauretania moored at a landing stage in Liverpool before World War I. The tiny figures give some idea of the impressive statistics of these great classic-age steamships.

Above: The French used Art Deco style for the Normandie and their other superliners, They used it with confidence and bravura, unlike the British who preferred to balance the old and the new and consequently fell before two stools.

The first-class dining salon of the S.S. France in 1928, The opulence and luxury is evident, though this form of decor would soon be consigned to history as ridiculously old-fashioned.

furniture in hotels. But whatever the styling it was done with panache and a reckless disregard of cost, and it must have seemed that the golden age of travel at sea was never-ending, with more and more people able to afford to travel in great comfort. The liners had a monopoly; there was no other way to cross the oceans.

The golden years abruptly ended with the tragic sinking of the British liner, *Titanic* on April 14th 1912 on her maiden voyage to New York. The ship that could not sink sank after a collision with an iceberg tore open the starboard side. Insufficient lifeboats meant that many would drown and the catalogue of errors ensured that the death toll topped 1500, including many Americans. Complacency had guaranteed that more attention had been given to surface gloss

rather than basic safety, and there was a level of incompetence amongst the senior crew that was staggering. There was also widespread disgust that almost until the last the third class passengers were segregated from the first class and were thus denied immediate access to the lifeboats. There were acts of great heroism, and also acts of gross selfishness and cowardice. It was a traumatic experience which the shipping companies took a long time to shake off, though the shipbuilders learned the lessons.

Surprisingly the ocean-going liners continued to operate during World War I, and were advertised blithely in the illustrated magazines as if there were no war on. It was fondly believed that no nation would sink a passenger vesse. Unquestionably the warring nations took advantage of this and despatched muni-

tions along with the travellers. This has been suggested as the reason why the Cunard's *Lusitania* was torpedoed off the coast of Ireland on May 8th 1915 by a German submarine with the loss of 1,198 lives, even though sufficient lifeboats had been provided in the wake of the tragedy of the *Titanic*. It has been speculated that this was one of the reasons why America entered the war against Germany, as many Americans were among the drowned. During World War I wholesale sinking of neutral and passenger liners was nowhere as systematic and ruthless as during World War II.

After World War I the German shipping industry was all but destroyed. Many liners, including the uncompleted *Bismarck*, were taken away as war reparations. Britain was traumatised by the war (a trauma which has never gone away), but the Americans flocked

to Britain and Europe as if things were back to normal. The 1920s brought in flippancy, a rather hysterical gaiety, the "flapper" society, and a decline in sexual morals. Transatlantic voyaging was openly seen as a chance to indulge oneself, and the "shipboard romance" became a cliché as well as a reality, an opportunity for professional gigolos to line their pockets at the expense of the vulnerable and rich.

If one golden age had ended, another started, even more dramatic than the heyday of the *Mauretania*. There was a new breed of transatlantic liners in a wholly new style; these were streamlined, eye-catching, often minimalist, and owed much to the rise of Art Deco, the name given to the new modern style inaugurated by the Exposition Internationale des Arts Decoratifs et Industriels Modernes, the exhibition held in

Above: The first-class ballroom of the M.S. Vulcania, decorated in rococo style.

Opposite: Ship interiors were often equipped and furnished to suit the passengers on particular steamship lines, and with the importance of the French colonies in Africa it is hardly surprising that the S.S. France had a Moorish room with members of the crew in ethnic costume.

Above: The Queen Elizabeth, among the last of the pre-war liners, with the new pattern of two funnels. Air travel was already threatening to make these floating hotels obsolete.

A striking but curiously incompetent advertisement of 1924 for the United American Lines and the Hamburg American Line, one of the most powerful steamship companies of the time, on a par with Cunard and White Star.

Paris in 1925. It is appropriate that the first liner wholly in this uncompromising style was *I'le de France*, launched in 1927, as the French were the acknowledged leaders in Art Deco. It became fashionable to travel on this new breed of liner, which included the German vessels *Bremen* – which took the Blue Riband from the *Mauretania* which had held it – and *Utopia* launched in 1928, but many seasoned travellers preferred the old style. Whatever their merits, the Art Deco liners were not cosy.

New facilities were demanded, including on-board cinemas, and there was a greater emphasis on activities that reflected the new age including swimming pools, both outdoor and indoor. Throughout the 1920s until the repeal of Prohibition in 1933 the bars offered welcome legal alcohol to American drinkers. The decks were large enough to

cater for sportsmen such as golfers, and if there was a demand for a particular activity it was provided. There were sports which were special to ocean liners, such as deck quoits, in which rope rings were thrown on upright pegs. A favourite activity amongst the active was jogging round the deck, circumnavigating the ship. There was tennis, shuffle-board, skeet shooting; French ships had bowling alleys and croquet courts. Gambling for large sums was commonplace and professional cardsharps found the transatlantic run highly lucrative The best chefs from Paris were enticed away to provide ever more exotic food.

Every ocean liner of any class had a first-rate orchestra and many professional dance-band musicians of note started their careers as "cocktail pianists". There was always ample staff, for, although there was a shortage of

*Those who have crossed more than once
invariably choose their ship with care*

S.S.
RELIANCE
ALBERT BALLIN

S.S.
RESOLUTE
DEUTSCHLAND

AND OTHER SPLENDID STEAMERS

UNITED AMERICAN LINES
(HARRIMAN LINE)
joint service with

HAMBURG AMERICAN LINE

Write for fascinating travel booklet P. Q.

39 BROADWAY, NEW YORK

CALVIN RAE SMITH
PARIS
1877

domestic labour in Britain and other countries, the glamour of working at sea was impossible to resist. Those travelling first class could feel that they had their own personal steward, solicitous and eager to please in the hope of a lavish tip. Amongst the crew there was a rigid hierarchy, and those at the bottom of the heap, the cleaners and the washers-up lived in the hidden depths of the ship in conditions not so different from the steerage passengers of the emigrant years. At the top was the captain and passengers vied for a place at his table at dinner – woe betide the captain who overlooked anyone important. The newsworthy passengers such as Charlie Chaplin disembarked surrounded by the world's press and the increasing hordes of newsreel photographers.

Writers found ship-life inspirational; Noel Coward's play *Private Lives* was written at sea, and Somerset Maugham admitted that he had got ideas for his fiction from overhearing bar-room conversations. Evelyn Waugh's The *Ordeal of Gilbert Pinfold* is probably the most intense and disturbing. In the environment of a liner the passenger was cocooned from real life, and those with mental health problems, like Gilbert Pinfold, were at their most vulnerable.

Not surprisingly, films and musicals were sometimes given an ocean-liner background. The most important was probably the Gershwin classic *Shall We Dance?* and

the most outlandish Sutton Vane's play *Outward Bound*, where all the passengers are dead, passing through purgatory. One answer to the popularity of an ocean-liner scenario is simple; the sets were easy to construct.

Art Deco was by no means a universal design style for liners. The Italian ships, passionately sponsored by Mussolini, were Renaissance palaces. The designers of the *Queen Mary*, launched in 1936, hedged their bets and timidly introduced Art Deco motifs where they were not offensive, and stylistically the *Normandie* of 1935, the most famous French liner of them all, showed a compromise compared with *I'le de France*, not sur-

Left: Brunel's mould-breaking The Great Western, showing the combination of sail and steam. Steamships had to be thoroughly established for the sails to be dispensed with. There was still a question mark about steam only when this painting was executed in about 1840.

Previous pages: Figures by moonlight on the deck watercolour by C. R. Smith, exploiting the romance of sea travel.

prisingly as the movement was running out of steam and had become a chainstore cliché.

Rivalry between the shipping lines was fierce, and there were relatively few of them – Cunard, P & O (Peninsular and Oriental), North German Lloyd, and what was known in America as the French line. In the 1840s Samuel Cunard had been subsidised by the British government, and passengers were supplemented by mail. In America, the Collins line of the 1840s had probably the best four ships in the world – the *Arctic*, *Atlantic*, *Baltic* and *Pacific*. The *Pacific* won the Blue Riband in 1851, averaging 13 knots across the Atlantic. The superliner was seen as a national status symbol. All the British and European vessels had state support of one kind or another, and all were heavily promoted.

There is no question that luxury sea travel was the most romantic form of travel, espe-

cially in the form of cruises, a speciality of the Italians who regarded the Mediterranean Sea as their own preserve. The organised chaos of embarkation and disembarkation was all part of the script, though it must have been a nightmare for colonial civil servants and their like who not only had to look after themselves but their furniture and effects as well.

The last superliner to be built before World War II was the *Queen Elizabeth I*, launched in 1938 and used as a troopship during the war. She was 1031 feet long, 118.5 feet broad, weighed 83,673 tons, and did good service before being retiring to Hong Kong in 1968 as an off-shore university. Unfortunately she a sank in 1972. The fate of many of the great liners was sad. At the outbreak of war the *Normandie* was ordered to stay in New York for safety's sake; after the surrender of France to Germany it was seized by the US govern-

Opposite: The opening of the Panama Canal in 1914 opened up great possibilities for the steamship companies, providing a sea link between the west and east coasts of America.

Below: The unspoken war between German and British shipping companies was no less aggressive than the build-up of naval forces prior to World War I. In the Kaiser Welhelm der Grosse, the Germans had a magnificent vessel, equipped and furnished regardless of expense.

Right: America had a network of short-haul steamship services, the Clyde Line being just one. Much of the traffic was between New York and the southern states. Although this advertisement dates from the turn of the century it depicts a steamship equipped with sails, with a tiny yacht in the foreground to give a misleading impression of great size.

Below: The Mauretania, sister ship of the ill-fated Lusitania, during her maiden voyage in 1907, a byword for luxury and a one-time holder of the Blue Riband, awarded to the ship which made the fastest Atlantic crossing.

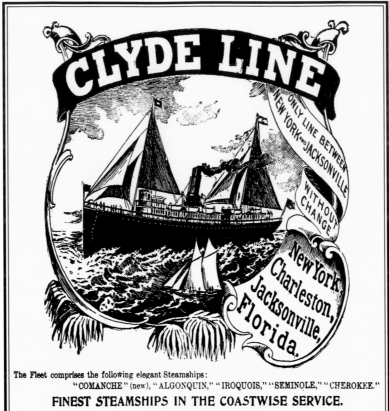

CLYDE LINE

ONLY LINE BETWEEN NEW YORK AND JACKSONVILLE WITHOUT CHANGE

New York, Charleston, Jacksonville, Florida.

The Fleet comprises the following elegant Steamships:
"COMANCHE" (new), "ALGONQUIN," "IROQUOIS," "SEMINOLE," "CHEROKEE."
FINEST STEAMSHIPS IN THE COASTWISE SERVICE.
Superb Passenger Accommodations.
Tables supplied with the best to be had in Northern and Southern Markets.
Tri-weekly Sailings from Pier 2? E. R., New York.
Write for new descriptive matter, rates, schedules, etc.
WM. P. CLYDE & CO., General Agents,
12 South Delaware Ave., Phila.   5 Bowling Green, N. Y.
M. H. CLYDE, Ass't Traffic M'g'r.   W. H. WARBURTON, East. Pass. Agt.
THEO. G. EGER. Traffic M'g'r. 5 BOWLING GREEN, N. Y.

ment. A fire and then flooding capsized her, huge crowds watched the attempts to raise her, but this failed and the hulk was sold for scrap. Other liners have taken on new roles. The *Queen Mary* ended up in America'a Long Beach in 1969 as a conference centre.

When the war ended it was hoped that the golden age would continue. The *United States* was the last word in luxury and speed, crossing the Atlantic in 1952 in three days ten hours, averaging an incredible 35 knots (41 mph.). The *Queen Elizabeth II* was launched to great acclaim in 1967, but by the time she went into service in 1969 she was virtually obsolete. Air travel had killed the superliner as a people carrier. But the

Right: The Mississippi paddle steamer Queen of the West, a lithograph by the American masters of the medium Currier and Ives. The Mississippi steamers were one of the first true luxury people carriers.

Previous pages: Embarkation scene by George Tuson (1853 - 1880), but such scenes were usually less decorous. Without the steamship mass emigration to America would have been impossible; many people sailed in frightful conditions, and it is impossible to say how many died in transit. Many had to provide their own food on embarking.

cruise lives on, if anything more popular than ever. It was believed that the days of the leviathan had gone for ever, that the monster ships of the past were industrial relics, suitable only for use as floating conference centres, but there are indications that seaborne cities are again on the agenda. Disneyland at sea, with acres of playspace, is the world of the immediate future. Unlike aircraft and trains, there is no limit to the size of a ship.

If ocean liners were the province of the rich and celebrated, the private yacht was originally the preserve of royalty, the nobility, and the well-connected, and amongst the cognoscenti it was considered vulgar to try and get from one place to another as quickly as possible. It was more important to travel than arrive.

The yacht was invented in Holland, used by the rich merchants to cruise the inland waterways and for sport – yacht is from a Dutch word, and with the word *Schip* added means "ship for chasing". The closest thing to a race was the chase, when several yachts pursued an imaginary enemy. English yachting began in 1660 when the city of Amsterdam presented King Charles II with a 66 foot (20 metre) yacht which he named *Mary*. Charles and his brother, later King James II, built other yachts and raced each other on the River Thames. Yachting became fashionable amongst the wealthy and the aristocracy, but the fashion was short-lived.

The first yacht club was formed about 1720 at Cork, Ireland, but the first English yacht club was Cowes in the Isle of Wight, dating from 1815 and still the most prestigious in Great Britain, jealously guarding its privileges and heritage. Sailing matches for large stakes were held, and yachts had to be at least 20 tons in weight (soon 200 tons would be normal). The Dutch brought yachting to America about the same time as it was introduced to Britain, but it was mostly recreational. Perhaps the first true luxury yacht was the American *Cleopatra's Barge* which cruised the Mediterranean in 1815, though the first American yacht club, the *Detroit,* was not started until 1839.

Until the second half of the nineteenth century yacht design was based on sailing ships such as brigantines and schooners, but in Cowes in 1851 the America, custom-designed, was triumphant. This was the start of the America's Cup, and organized international racing. Long-distance yachting was marked in 1895-98 by the first single-handed voyage round the world. Luxury yachting was the prerogative of power yachts, first of all steam yachts with paddle wheels, then propellers, followed by gasoline and diesel engines in the twentieth century. Power yachts could be larger; the *Mayflower* (1897) was the official yacht of the President of the United States and weighed 2690 tons. Manned by a crew of 150 it was incredibly long lasting and saw service in World War II. Although tiny compared with the ocean liners, these large power yachts, culminating in the *Orion* (1930) of 3097 tons, contained many features associated with liners, and although the building of large power yachts declined after 1932 partly on the grounds of expense, the pastime grew in popularity, especially amongst those who liked coastal and inland waterway cruising. Many saw the sails as irrelevant and a mere nuisance, and the cabin cruiser came into its own, needing a smaller crew and less expertise. After World War II ex-naval vessels came on to the market, ripe for conversion, and often there was not only romance but positive danger as eccentric vessels took to sea. Messing about in boats took on a new meaning.

The centre of pleasure yachting was the Mediterranean Sea, but travelling was often less important than being seen in the up-market harbours and marinas. Much of this was true about ocean liners as well. The journeying was only incidental.

ORIENT LINE
BETWEEN
LONDON AND AUSTRALIA

THE ORIENT LINE

is under contract with the Commonwealth Government of Australia for a fortnightly Mail Service between England and Australia.

THE ROUTE

followed is by way of Gibraltar, South of France, Naples, Egypt and Ceylon ; the ports in Australia visited being Fremantle, Adelaide, Melbourne, Sydney and Brisbane.

THE PASSENGER ACCOMMODATION

includes cabins de luxe, bedstead state rooms and single berth cabins. There are luxurious lounges, music saloons, electric elevators and laundries. The steamers are fitted with wireless telegraphy.

THE STEAMERS

are amongst the finest and largest running East of Suez.

Managers :
F. GREEN & Co.
ANDERSON, ANDERSON & Co.

Head Offices—FENCHURCH AVENUE, LONDON, E.C.
West End Branch Office—28, COCKSPUR STREET, S.W.
Telephone Number: CITY 3000.   Cable Address: " ANDERSONS, LONDON."
Telegrams, Inland: " ANDERSONS, TELEW, LONDON."

*B*Y *A*IR

In the 15 years from the Wright Brother's first flight to the end of World War I the airplane developed from a thing of strings and wire to an engineering marvel. After the war the potential for air travel was speedily seen and in 1919 the London – Paris service, pioneered by the Aircraft Travel and Transport Company, began operations from Hounslow aerodrome just outside London. The company ran two seaters and four seaters, with windows that the passengers could open or shut. Communication between the pilot and the passengers was by passing notes through a trap door in a partition behind his head. The first scheduled air line, however, was German, operating from February 1919 from Berlin to Leipzig and Weimar.

The journey between Paris and London could be uncomfortable as the planes could not ascend above the "weather", most of which occurs below 4000 feet. The passengers were an optional extra; the service was basically intended for mail. Important travellers such as Winston Churchill travelled by De Havilland D.H.4As operated by the Royal Air Force. This special squadron was disbanded in 1919, and the aircraft, along with hundreds of warplanes, were sold to Handley Page Ltd, one of the four main post-war air lines. The others were Instone Air Line Ltd., Daimler Airways, and British Marine Air Navigation Company, later merging to form Imperial Airways Ltd., the main UK air line, forcibly merged with other air lines and nationalised in 1938 after irregularities and resulting in British Airways. This became BOAC in 1939, with BEA (British European Airways) split off in 1946 to form a separate company.

There was widespread reluctance to fly, but potential passengers were lured by cheap joy rides at aerodromes, where the pilots were ex-Royal Air Force fliers using old planes, especially the Avro 504K wooden trainers, which would otherwise have been scrapped. At a guinea (£1.05) a time, these were enormously popular. One of

Above: For many years the future of air transport was seen in airships.

Opposite: The interior of an unknown airplane of about 1927 entitled "Luxury in Air Travel" though it seems more like a commuter's nightmare.

and London to Paris was two hours forty-five minutes. One Paris to London trip took one hour forty-five minutes with the help of a 100 mph hurricane. The passengers, well-fuelled with brandy, thought the turbulence was due to the pilot's stunt flying. Adventurous as these trips were, they were not economically viable, and it was reckoned that a minimum of twelve passengers were needed. There was also increasing competition from foreign air lines, especially the Dutch air line KLM (the oldest existing air line) who used reliable German Fokkers. The Dutch considered it was not safe to fly the North Sea so initially they hugged the coast and crossed the English Channel.

Although the American Glenn H. Curtiss had been experimenting with powerful aircraft engines from 1911, the Americans were late on the scene. Domestic air lines were

Above: Wilbur and Orville Wright in 1910.

Opposite: The Wright brothers testing their new airplane in North Carolina in 1903.

the most successful was at Blackpool, Lancashire, where five pilots carried 10,000 passengers over two months (42 trips in a ten-hour day). There were no accidents. Early air travel was advertised as safe, and it was safe. Cobham's Flying Service became famous in the 1920s, charging five shillings (25p) for a flight over south Wales.

The scheduled time from Paris to London

not proposed until 1926. Pan American Airways was founded in 1927 and went out of business in 1991. Transcontinental flights were fraught with difficulties. Flying over mountains was difficult if not impossible, and the Appalachians were a block. In comparison, European travel was easy – flat terrain and short stretches of sea.

More passengers meant larger aircraft, and

Right: Zeppelin LZ - 4 on a trial flight over Bodensee in Switzerland in 1908. In a few years the Zeppelins struck terror in the hearts of the English with their bombing raids during World War I, though once located they were easily shot down.

An Imperial Airways flying boat of 1934. Imperial Airways was the direct ancestor of the British national airline, though without the trials and tribulations that afflicted BEA and BOAC and, their successor, British Airways.

preferably more powerful engines, and there was also the question of needing longer runways. Most runways were no more than 1000 feet in length, and aerodromes (not yet called airports) were criss-crossed with runways as airplanes had to land against the prevailing wind. The answer seemed to be the flying boat where there was no limit for take off and landing. The Americans even tried developing "tamed" ocean, but this was not a success. The flying boat, a great success story, reached its apotheosis with Howard Hughes gargantuan Goose, obsolete whilst on the drawing-board.

Early travellers were mainly business men or adventurers. There were few women and hardly any children. They did not expect luxury and did not get it. Hounslow airfield,

used until 1920, had no refreshment facilities, though Croydon, London's new civil airport, had a hotel and a restaurant. Until 1921 no meteorological information was available; the pilot found what the weather was like by being in it. There was not the volume of traffic on the Paris-London run that was predicted, and several companies vied for custom. The British companies were subsidised by the state to ensure their participation in potentially the most lucrative route.

The only way was to attract the wealthy. This meant comfort, luxury, safety, smooth flying, ample toilet facilities, good food in transit, and it did not mean flying boats unless they were allowed to put down on the Seine. The first to pioneer in-flight lavatories were the British; the credit for in-flight meals goes to the French, with initially pre-cooked food heated in flight, and hot drinks in Thermos flasks. From the late 1920s there was a massive effort in the US to increase the number of airports due to a powerful pressure group, the National Aeronautics Association. Gradually the Americans became the premier flying nation, and Douglas and Boeing began to produce the aircraft all the world wanted, though the workhorse of the 1920s was the now forgotten Ford Trimotor. 1930 saw the introduction of the all-metal Boeing Monomail with the novelty of retractable undercarriage. 1933 heralded the appearance of the Douglas DC 1, the forerunner of the DC 3, the Dakota (13,000 made) and the two-engined Boeing 247, which foreshadowed the later Boeing giants, the 727 and 747.

These planes were still not large enough, and would not be until four-engined planes became the norm, able to fly above the weather. Air lines used snob appeal to increase passengers, drawing attention to film stars, millionaires and royalty who had travelled with them. Silver Wing Travel was a division of Imperial Airways, with its own soothing soft-sell. "Really, it is like nothing so much as sitting in the armchair of a Pullman car which suddenly takes to itself wings." For safety, "Outside you can hear the hum of the three giant engines, any two of which would bear you safely to your destination." Three engines was a good compromise between two and four. The celebrated long-lived

German Junkers G-31 which later developed into the JU-52, used for dropping paratroops in World War II, is perhaps the best-known three-engined plane. Silver Wing three-engined aircraft carried thirty-eight passengers. The cost was half as much again from London to Paris as the tiresome sea and rail service. There was also the Paris Shopping Special, back in a few hours with plenty of time for lunch at Maxim's.

Patronage by royalty was always worth a

Below: Passengers arriving at Croydon after their flight from Le Bourget, Paris, and being checked through customs. At this time, 1921, Croydon was still a place of huts and shacks, and until the building of Heathrow was London's main airport.

plug. "We had the distinction of carrying on the Cairo-Basra service H.M. King Feisal and the Emir Ghazi of Iraq", proclaimed Imperial Airways. It was not called Imperial Airways for nothing. It went everywhere, though crossing the Atlantic, with its lack of stop-overs, was still fraught with difficulty, even though it had been done in 1919 by a US Navy NC-4 via the Azores and later by Lindbergh in his absurdly tiny *Spirit of St Louis*.

The Germans considered that they had the answer to transatlantic flight – the Zeppelin. The first airship had been built in France in 1852 with a three hp steam engine, which covered 20 miles from Paris at six mph (20 km). The first German Zeppelin dates from 1900. During World War I the Zeppelin was used to bomb Britain, suicide missions as air-ships were big, slow, and, if the searchlights could find them, easily shot down. The Graf Zeppelin was built in 1928 and during its period of service until 1937 it flew 590 flights including 144 ocean crossings. Fifty passengers were carried on the Atlantic run; otherwise it was 150. The Zeppelin was 420 feet (128m) long, powered with two 16 horsepower engines, it made 20 miles per hour and thus the Atlantic was a long but comfortable haul as the passengers were transported in great luxury. The Hindenburg was twice as big, had four 1100 hp engines, and was four times as fast. In 1936 it carried 1002 passengers on ten flights Germany – United States. The airship with its volatile fuel (hydrogen) was a lighter-than-air bomb, and tragedies such as the crash of the Hindeburg itself in 1937 whilst landing at Lakehurst, New Jersey, with the loss of 36 lives, and the tragic crash of the British R-101 in France took the rigid airship out of contention.

Business passengers were the bread and butter of the industry. They were interested in speed not comfort. Jockeys, surgeons, and musicians also wanted speed. Steve Donoghue the famous jockey of the 1920s rode in a two o'clock race at Windsor in

Left: A De Haviland airplane of the 1920s, carrying ten passengers. Unless the aircraft were privately hired, this was not an economic number except for short joy-rides. Two-engined warplanes had been used in World War I and developments of these provided the first multi-engined passenger planes.

Overleaf: A Transatlantic flying boat moored to a buoy. These flying boats contained accommodation on two levels, but they were necessarily slow and eventually they disappeared, though during World War II their great range made them ideal for anti-submarine warfare.

HYDRAVION
TRANSATLANTIQUE LAT

37 TONNES

Geo Ham

England and a four-thirty race at Ostend, Belgium, on the same day. A four-seater plane cost £25 a mile to hire.

Aerodromes with shacks and hangers became airports. The government paid-for Croydon Airport opened in 1928 with facilities akin to a first-rate railway station (though it was always inferior to continental airports), but on aircraft there were still notices saying that it was forbidden to throw anything out of the windows. Noise was still loud, and passengers were supplied with cotton-wool plugs to stuff into their ears. As is now politically correct but then wasn't, smoking was not allowed. In 1936 an Englishman was successfully prosecuted for smoking on board plane. Stewards provided brown paper bags for what the French elegantly described as pour le mal de l'air. The Americans introduced stewardesses in 1930 on the United Airlines, and their soothing presence provided nervous passengers with a feeling of safety.

Deutsche Lufthansa had introduced stewards in the 1920s; Lufthansa was the first air line to provide genuine hot meals in flight, and were pioneers in providing fully reclining seats for night journeys. The down-side of increasingly popular air travel was the division between first-class and second-class passengers; the second-class had older and slower aircraft and less luxury.

In the late 1920s the US Transcontinental Air Transport (later Trans-World Airlines) established a coast-to-coast link across the continent in 48 hours using train and plane, cut to 36 hours by 1930 with no rail travel but an overnight stop in Kansas City. TWA conquered night flying in 1932 and the trip could be made in 24 hours, strong competition for the railroad operators. The rivalry between rail and air was responsible for dramatic progress in pleasurable travel in the US, hardly matched elsewhere. TWA pioneered safety belts for landing and take-off; the days were gone when passengers could be hurtled down an aisle by an unforeseen air current.

Although Igor Sikorski, the Russian-born

Left: The Graf Zeppelin being towed out of its shed. The best known of all airships, it was believed to be the ideal people-carrier, and the luxury offered could not be matched by fixed-wing aircraft. It is still believed that there is a future for the airship, especially with the development of non-inflammable gas.

Left: A hectic scene at Croydon Airport in the 1920s with a French Bleriot 165 (foreground) and a Brequet 280T, painted by Kenneth McDonough.

Left: The Maia-Mercury "piggy-back" composite aircraft was a short-lived development of the flying boat. The flying boat offered luxury unknown in ordinary air liners, with cabins instead of cramped seats. Their great disadvantage was that they could not serve inland cities.

American aeronautical engineer, had built and flown the first four-engined plane, the Bolsche, in 1913 (and invented the first helicopter in 1941), it was not a realistic proposition until powerful engines came into being. When Pan American sought to open a service from California to the Philippines and China it faced a stage of 2400 miles to Honolulu, and in 1932 Sikorski was commissioned to provide a four-engined flying boat. In the same year the aviation company Glenn Martin was commissioned to make an even bigger plane weighing 26 tons and it was the Martin M-130, the China Clipper, that made the first airmail flight across the Pacific in 1935. The wingspan of the Clipper was 130 feet (equal to the Boeing 727). In 1936 passengers were carried as well as mail.

To "fly above the weather" meant that pressurised cabins were necessary, and if planes could operate at great height there would be less turbulence and greater fuel economy. The first hurdle was developing an airtight cabin, but eventually all the difficulties were conquered and the Boeing Stratoliner came into being in 1940, capable of flying at 14,000 feet at 200 mph. During World War II it was the only commercial airplane to fly directly from Newfoundland to Northern Ireland. Just before the war the DC-3 was enlarged to take four engines, but it was not pressurised and the design was obsolete.

In the 1930s colonial routes were all important. Most of the European powers had colonies, and this simplified the business of getting landing rights. The sky was dominated by three air lines, Pan American, Imperial Airways, and the Dutch KLM, and landing rights were settled amicably. In America, flying was regarded as no more extravagant than travelling by rail but in Britain and most of Europe only the wealthy flew (in Britain there were few airports and those that were in existence were in city outskirts – it was quicker by train), though where there were

Opposite: On May 6th 1937 the future of the airship was clouded by the explosion of the Hindenburg while landing in New Jersey. The equally tragic end of the British R-101 some years earlier had already posed a question mark over the airship.

Right: Indeed a home from home, an interior of a Fokker airliner.

Opposite top: This photograph was taken in 1919, when air travel was for diplomacy and business rather than pleasure.

Opposite: below: This photograph shows two intrepid ladies boarding the venerable Vickers Vimy.

Below: The first inkling of the great age of mass travel, a Pan-American Lockheed Constellation at London's Heathrow in 1947.

great distances to cover even the timorous conquered their reservations, and SAS (in Norway, Sweden and Denmark) and Aeroflot in Russia profited.

It was essential to get women to fly. "Your complexions will not suffer during air travel", promised Imperial Airways, "for one of the greatest features of flight is that everything is so clean – no dust, no dirt, you look, and are, as cool and fresh on arrival as when you started." There was so much to interest children that they never had time to cry, or so the advertising went. Imperial Airways were aware that flying was still a mystery. "There's absolutely no need for furs, goggles, or special gloves". It must have worked as air package holidays were projected in 1939, though not carried out because of World War II.

Faster travel times meant cutting down on some luxuries. The five-course Imperial Airways meal gave way to snacks when London to Paris took an hour and ten minutes, and the airline gave up the practice of issuing passengers with maps with a black line to mark their route. There was enterprise – the Tea Flight over London while a "dainty tea" is consumed, thirty minutes, £1.10 shillings a head (£1.50). Swissair did consumer research in 1933. No air sickness recorded, while even the most corpulent of passengers (eighteen and a half stone) had plenty of room alongside his three neighbours.

The American air lines were constantly trying for new customers. Pan American provided free socks with cardboard soles to prevent passengers' feet swelling during flight, and the Douglas Sleeper Transport provided two-tier berths of great comfort for their overnight services. The safety record was so impressive that Hollywood decreed that their actors and actresses were now able to travel by air. The Douglas DC-3 provided radio for its passengers with "individual loudspeakers".

In remote parts of the world, any kind of

Left: A Westland airplane taking off from Croydon about 1930, interesting because of the grand structure of Croydon Airport itself in the background, with its restaurants, hotels, and administrative blocks.

*Left: An Imperial
Airways flying boat, the
Golden Hind, taking off,
an impressive spectacle,
a reminder of an age
when travel was often
better than arriving,
customs was an amiable
formality and there were
actually porters to help
with the luggage.*

Left: The cabin of the Imperial Airways Atlanta in the mid 1930s, showing the luxury that was offered - at a price. The days had gone when passengers were urged not to hurl things out of the window and hot drinks were provided from a Thermos flask.

air travel no matter how uncomfortable was worth it. Passengers were often crammed in with cargo, and often obliged to help with unloading or pushing the plane into the air current before taking off. In Australia, no-one would insure passengers on the airline Qantas, and they signed their tickets declaring that they were travelling at their own risk. It was the romance of travel pushed to its limits. In Russia the planes were incredibly slow, averaging 54 mph on domestic routes; as late as 1934 it took eleven hours to fly from Moscow to Berlin.

Long-distance travel could seem endless. With its various stops, London to Capetown took ten days in 1933. Some air lines such as KLM reduced the number of passengers on their planes so that they would travel in comfort. Even in hostile surroundings few aircraft crashed. When a passenger noted that part of the aircraft wing had broken off he wanted to photograph it, but was persuaded not to by the pilot who told him that it was "not good advertising for flying".

Except for the Zeppelins, probably the most luxurious travel was provided by the Empire, Ensign, and Imperial flying boats, where the accommodation was in cabins. The steward's kitchen, wrote one traveller, "is a perfect example for any kitchen planning expert". Central heating was done by steam, a range of snacks was free on request, and playing cards, crossword puzzles, jigsaw puzzles, books, and magazines were provided by the management. Fully carpeted, with a promenade deck, sumptuous meals – this must have been truly the golden age of air travel for those who did not have their own private plane.

After World War II air travel became the norm for those previously earthbound. The first pure-jet commercial plane, the de Havilland Comet, entered service in 1952. Supersonic travel arrived with the Concorde in 1976. There is still romance for those who seek it and can afford to pay for it. For others, the romance lies in wait at the end of their journey. Which may last longer than they want.

Opposite: The interior of an Armstrong-Whitworth Argosy in 1927, hardly a model of comfort, and newcomers to flying must have wondered what they had let themselves in for, though at least the cabin had a fire extinguisher.

HOTELS AND RESTAURANTS

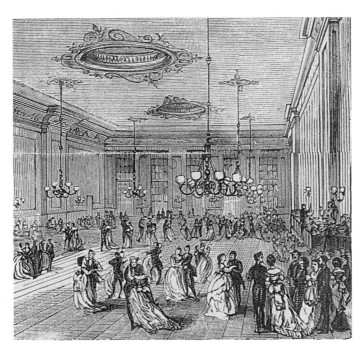

The coming of rail marked the demise of the coaching inn, though many struggled on, hoping that local custom would keep them going, though the lucrative stage-coach stops, especially if they were overnight, made this difficult. A new form of accommodation arose which rapidly assumed a dominating role – the railway hotel. Although there had been important hotels in the great cities, especially London, for some years, they catered for a superior class of person. As late as the 1880s ladies, even married women, did not mix with the *hoi polloi* in hotel dining rooms, and either the rooms had a dining room or meals were brought up to them, but the railway hotel, whose patrons were usually the prosperous middle classes – the poor may make day excursions and seaside trips but they did not use hotels – and these men and women, many of whom rose from humble beginnings, were far more free and broad-minded in their attitudes.

The railway proprietors quickly saw the opportunities offered by the new rich breed of travellers, and when the great stations were built they included huge hotels, so that when passengers arrived they were met by hotel porters and conveyed straight away to their hotel room. Some hoteliers not associated with the railroad but seeing the possibilities aimed their advertising at rail passengers. Typical of these was Ham's Royal Western Hotel in Bristol, which suffered the disadvantage of being some distance from the station. Ham's offered "superior accommodation in Suites of Apartments handsomely fitted up and combining every comfort for Families, with Coffee and Commercial Rooms not surpassed by any House in the Kingdom, to which the travelling Community are respectfully solicited. Baths, Warm, Cold, Vapour and Shower, in the House. Omnibuses to and from every Train." All well and good, but a hotel adjacent to the rail station was far preferable.

Among the first railroad hotels was the Grosvenor, built at Victoria Station at 1839. The London and

Above: The ballroom at the Grand Union hotel Saratoga.

Opposite: The Palm Court of the Ritz hotel, London, one of the great prestige hotels of all time.

Birmingham Railway was opened in 1838, and the Euston and Victoria Hotels were built on either side of the entrance, opened in 1840 by a hotel company composed principally of shareholders of the railroad company. These hotels were let to the company on a twenty-one year lease, so that theoretically the railroad and the hotel were separate entities, though they were in fact closely associated.

In 1854 the Great Western Royal Hotel was opened at Paddington. "Passengers by the Trains can pass between the Platforms and the Hotel at once, without trouble or expense, and proper persons will always be in attendance to receive and carry the Luggage to and from the Trains." Passengers were advised to book their rooms in advance by letter, or by telegram (paid for by the railroad company). This was usual in the best central London hotels. Claridge's, one of the most prestigious of the London hotels, required references before they granted strangers access to their services.

At the Great Western Royal Hotel guests were charged extra for baths (two and sixpence – 12p – for hot baths, one and six – 7p – for cold baths). Taking a bath was more expensive than taking a bedroom on the fourth floor. Food was extra, as were cups of tea and coffee (sixpence – 2p), extraordinarily expensive. Forty cups of tea equalled a labourer's weekly wage.

Some of the early railroad directors still thought in stage-coach terms, and a large hotel was built at Slough, once an important staging post 18 miles from London. It was overlooked that Slough was only half an hour away by train from the prestigious London railroad hotels, and the hotel rapidly went bankrupt. Existing hoteliers and innkeepers often resorted to law to stop the building of railroad hotels and litigation sometimes went on for years. But nothing could stop the spread. In 1863 the Charing Cross Hotel was opened, and in 1865 the St Pancras Hotel. In the streets by the great stations smaller hotels, known as family or commercial, were opened,

Left: The Cambridge Telegraph stagecoach outside the White Horse Tavern and Family Hotel about 1835 when it was still believed that this form of transport had a future.

*Right: The Great
Western Hotel,
Paddington, in 1852, one
of the first of the great
London railway hotels,
built by the celebrated
architect P. Hardwick in
what was a typical rail-
way style - grand,
imposing, and echoing
the majesty of the
railway revolution.*

varying from the modestly comfortable to the
appalling.

The United States, many countries in
Europe, and Britain were following the same
route, though in America the hotels were larger with more amenities. Even in the best
British hotels bathrooms were often few and
far between, and the patrons had to make do
with a hip bath kept under the bed into
which was emptied a jug of hot water and a
jug of cold by the servants. The Glasgow St.
Enoch's Hotel (1876) had 200 bedrooms on
five floors, while the North British Station
Hotel (1902) of Edinburgh claimed to be one
of the largest and most palatial in Europe
with 257 bedrooms, 14 public rooms, nine
private sitting rooms, 52 bathrooms, and opu-
lent suites of rooms. By this time, elevators
were used in the more adventurous hotels.
Some of the hotels had ballrooms and ban-
queting rooms, and became the social and
business centres of the towns and cities, but
times and tastes change, and the active life of
these monster hotels was often not long. St
Pancras, the most spectacular of them all,
closed in 1935.

Eye-catching as the railroad hotels were,
they could not compete in comfort and prestige with the best inner-city London hotels,
which had often been built for visiting royalty
who had nowhere else to stay. In the early
nineteenth century the hotels in the West End
of London had been opened by French chefs
who had been working in England and
retired butlers who knew the ways of the
upper classes. The cuisine of the station
hotels was usually mundane but the private
hotels provided the best and the adventurous.
There was fierce competition between the
hotels, and constant innovation, with the
Savoy Hotel in London stealing a march on its
rivals in 1889 by providing electricity from its
own generators, but by close attention to the
needs of regular guests the most profitable
hotels truly made visitors feel thoroughly at
home – and made certain that fellow guests
were in the same mould. This snobbery was

*Overleaf: At the time,
1874, the Grand Union
hotel Saratoga, boasted
of being the largest hotel
in the world, and cer-
tainly the hotels of the
United States dwarfed
those in Europe, except
in Russia. Some of the
hotels turned out to be
too large, or located in
the wrong place - the
railroad companies were
sometimes too optimistic.*

OS CHALÊTS.

VISTA DA VARANDA.

ESCADA E ASCENSOR.

O ESCRIPTORIO.

UM PATEO INTERIOR.

A SALA DA DANSA.

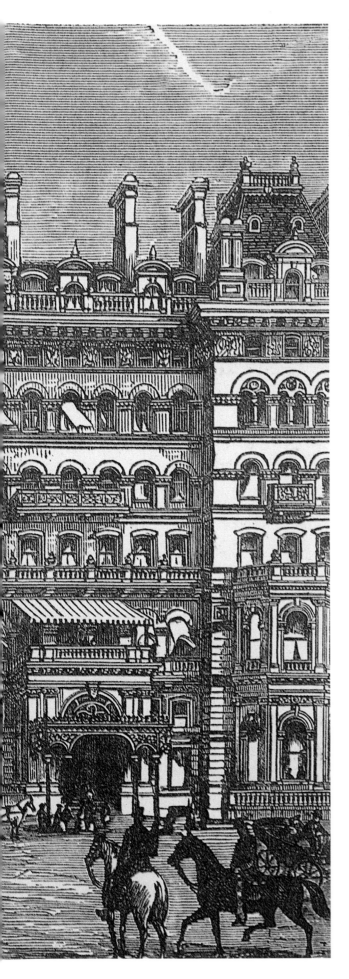

not confined to Britain. The proprietor of perhaps the best-known hotel in the world, the Ritz of Paris, deliberately avoided having a "lounge", though there were reading, writing and waiting rooms, because he wanted "to avoid undesirable presences", though maybe this was shorthand for wanting to keep prostitutes away.

Throughout their life-spans hotels were constantly altered and up-graded to suit the fickle tastes of the guests, and they often absorbed buildings on either side. This happened with the Ritz Paris, creating great confusion for guests who were constantly lost in the maze of unexpected corridors. Losing one's way was a social gaffe, and regulars could hardly contain their glee as they piloted some unfortunate to civilization.

London was the largest city in the world – three times the size of New York – and despite hectic construction there were always insufficient quality hotels to cope with the millions of visitors from the 1850s onwards. The Langham Hotel (projected 1858, opened in 1865) was typical of the new breed of monster hotels and one of the largest buildings in London, with a frontage of 200 feet, 120 feet high, six stories, and with 600 apartments. Besides the usual dining rooms and drawing rooms, it had billiards rooms, its own post office and telegraph office, a parcels office, and an elevator "which goes up and down at intervals". Elevators, known in Britain as lifts, were still novel enough to merit an explanation. The Langham closed at the outbreak of World War II and it was taken over as offices; part of it was used by the British Broadcasting Corporation.

Large as it was, the Langham was dwarfed by many contemporary American hotels such as the Palace in San Francisco. After World War I US hotels were aspiring to small towns. The largest hotel in the world, the Stevens hotel in Chicago (later the Conrad Hilton) had 3000 rooms. The hotel lost out in size to the Hotel Rossiya in Moscow in the late 1960s. There is a simple reason why

Left: When it was built, Langham Hotel in Portland Place, London, was a wonder of the age, dwarfing almost every other hotel in London and offering facilities previously unheard of. It had its own post office, and in appearance it was more of a palace than a hotel.

*Right: The Great
Northern Hotel in Hot
Springs National Park,
Arkansas, about 1928.
During this period hotels
not only catered for train
travellers and "the car-
riage trade" but increas-
ingly for motorists from
every walk of life, for
some of whom hotels
were a mystery and
remained so.*

American hotels were so much larger than
British and European hotels – the skyscraper
and accommodation on numerous floors.
They were also part of combines with massive
finance, permitting bulk buying and extensive
advertising campaigns empasising the "family"
link between individual hotels. In 1908 the
Statler Hotel opened in Buffalo, New Jersey,
and Ellsworth Milton Statler introduced many
innovations and conveniences especially for
the growing and increasingly influential business traveller. The Statler Company was the
first great chain operation in hotelkeeping.

The most prestigious hotels were much
smaller than the Langham. The Paris Ritz had
210 rooms, and the Savoy, managed confus-
ingly by César Ritz with the great Auguste
Escoffier as his chef, opened in 1889 on the
profits of the Gilbert and Sullivan operas
staged at the Savoy Theatre next door, was
also modest in size, as were the London Ritz
and Carlton, and the venerable and civilized
Brown's of Dover Street (opened in 1837 and
still going strong). Where the facilities offered
were more or less equal, the quality of the
cuisine was all important, and here Escoffier
was supreme, bringing in a Viennese baker to
help provide the best bread, unsurpassed in
presentation at the table, conjuring up novel
sauces, and inventing dishes for important
guests, such as the Prince of Wales (frogs' legs
in a cream jelly). All diners were obliged to
wear full evening dress; to keep out the riff-
raff Ritz kept a stock of "reserved" notices for
empty tables. When dinners often ran to ten
courses, the kitchen staff were, to say the least
of it, worked hard.

As famous in her day as Ritz was Rosa
Lewis who ran the Cavendish, a "private"
hotel with no public rooms or even a dining
room. Meals were carried in great ceremony
to the guests' rooms. Although it was 1902
there were only three bathrooms and no telephone, but writing in 1923 she declared that
there were now 46 "and we are no happier
with the 46 than we were with the three!"
Rosa Lewis was known as the "Queen of

*Overleaf: The lobby of a
New York hotel about
1895, drawn by the
great English artist Phil
May. The spaciousness of
the New York hotel is
evident and May intro-
duces a convincing
bunch of guests.*

WINTER SPORTS of every kind at ST. MORITZ (Engadine), **6000** ft. above Sea, in brilliant sunshine, and in dry, exhilarating, health-giving air.

The Finest Family Hotel for Wintering in Switzerland is the

Grand Hotel St. Moritz

Large Private Ice Rink.

Skiing, Tobogganing, &c.

First Opened December, 1905.

300 Rooms Warmed by Hot Water.

Latest Sanitary Arrangements by a Leading English Firm.

Private Orchestra for Concerts and Balls.

Write to THE MANAGER for Illustrated Prospectus and Tariff.

Engadine Express Train three times weekly from Calais to St. Moritz.

Above: First opened in 1905, the Grand Hotel, St Moritz, had 300 rooms with trains three days a week to Calais. The railroad opened up the winter sports scene to a new generation.

Cooks" and was highly praised by Escoffier. She was the subject of a major British television series, *Duchess of Duke Street*.

With the constant expansion of the railways, sleepy seaside resorts became fashionable towns, often promoted for their believed medicinal properties. Torquay in Devon, England, was typical. Before the railroad arrived in 1858, the total number of rooms available to visitors was around 500 , including those in lodging houses. It was decided to build a large hotel, a concept so revolutionary that almost until it was opened in 1868 it was simply known as "The Hotel". Named the Imperial, it boasted of probably "the finest cuisine outside London", and no expense was spared in its construction though initially it only had 50 rooms. Torquay tried to vie with the French Riviera, and tables were published showing that temperatures were higher in Torquay – in winter. Winter was the fashionable season. Guests had the gratification of seeing their names published in the local paper. Torquay was typical of up-market seaside resorts, though eventually it was faced with the ancient problem as to whether to cater for the cream of society or, with the growth of the motor car, mass tourism (mass tourism won).

Railroad companies did not lack initiative, and promoted remote beauty spots (such as the Lake District in England), building railroads just for tourism. Much the same happened in America and throughout Europe. And where the railroads penetrated, high-class hotels were sure to follow. With the pre-

occupation with health amongst the rich (though they simply should have eaten less), the rail gave easy access to spa towns such as Tunbridge Wells, which boasted one of the grandest hotels outside London, and Baden-Baden in Germany. Sometimes the rail companies overestimated the potential demand; some locations did not live up to their promise. Sometimes railroads were built for "social" reasons, and lost money year after year, though many survived until the 1960s when the railroads were subjected to strict commercial scrutiny throughout the western world.

As railroads were opened throughout the world (Japan 1872, Persia 1873, China 1877) hotels sprang up, sometimes in national styles, sometimes in an international style, not only for overseas travellers but for businessmen and merchants, and many of these

became famous, such as the Raffles Hotel in Singapore, which was a home-from-home amongst British expatriates. The Grand at Monte Carlo, the National at Lucerne, the Hotel de Provence at Cannes, all attracted the royalty and aristocracy of all Europe, and many of them were supervised by César Ritz. Some of these hotels were brave adventures into the unknown, built where nobody much had been and where nobody would come. The Indian hotels were modelled on princely palaces, and where there was plenty of space hotels were built in just one storey. The British were still the greatest trading nation in the world, and their travel requirements were studiously taken into consideration.

One of the pleasures of travel was food, supplied by the hotels or restaurants. The first restaurant was opened in Paris by A. Boulanger, a soup vendor, in 1765; a sign

Above: The Hotel d'Europe in St Petersburg, Russia, in the late nineteenth century, a mammoth building serving one of the most sophisticated cities in Europe, and until the technological advances of the nineteenth century in steam and rail largely unknown to the English and the Americans.

over his door advertised restoratives or *restaurants,* and the name stuck throughout Europe, with slight variations (*restoran* in Russia). The first luxury restaurant opened in Paris in 1782, and the owner wrote *L'Art du Cuisinier* (1814) a cookery book that became the bible of the restaurant industry, and industry it was especially in Paris after the French Revolution

when chefs and cooks who had served the old aristocracy opened their own eating establishments. By 1804 Paris had more than 500 restaurants, producing many famous chefs who evolved dishes that have since remained classics. A typical restaurant listed a dozen soups, two dozen fish dishes, fifteen beef entrées, 20 mutton entrées, and scores of side

dishes. The novelist Honoré de Balzac who habitually dined at the Véry restaurant often went through the card. The most famous Paris restaurant was the Café Anglais, which closed in 1913, overtaken in renown by Maxim's.

Although it is widely believed that the British had only chop-houses where the food was thrown at one and American food was disowned even by its creators, this is not true. London had many specialized eating-houses, one of them, surprisingly, for curry, though the "leg of mutton" syndrome was widespread and it is not to be wondered at that so much reverence was paid to the French restaurants and why London hotels employing French chefs were so highly rated.

Right: The Hotel Cecil in London painted by R. S. Pike in 1931, the golden age of the well off and for whom the grand hotels of London assiduously catered , though the Hotel Cecil was exceptional with its marvellous views across the River Thames.

Opposite: Entrepreneurs of nations striving to attract tourists built the hotels they thought would please; some chose an international style, some a style which would reflect their country as here, the Hotel Shah Abbas, Isfahan, Iran.

Overleaf: The Casino, Monte Carlo, to which the world's gamblers flocked by land, sea and air.

The chefs developed the *brigade de cuisine*, or kitchen team, consisting of highly trained experts each with clearly defined duties. It was possible to avoid over-lapping in the days when meals were consumed over several hours. The willingness of the French to consider cuisine an art form was widely scoffed at but equally widely copied. The prestige of French cooking did much to check national dishes into the present century, except in America, apart from the south, such as in New Orleans, where there was a strong French influence, and possibly Scandinavia. The Americans themselves had a deep influence on world cuisine, especially fast-food outlets. The cafeteria originated in San Francisco during the 1849 gold rush, though it took many years for it to be adopted in Britain and Europe though the buffets on railroad stations prepared the way.

World War I was a watershed for both railroads and hotels, and many hotels failed to move with the times, including the Cavendish which though frequented by the Prince of Wales, later Edward VIII, was well past its best. In 1932 the novelist Aldous Huxley stayed there, and found it "like staying in a run-down country house – large comfortable rooms, but everything a bit shabby and a bit dirty." Some hotels survived through character alone, such as Brown's, which had much the atmosphere of a superior gentleman's club. The Cavendish amazingly survived until 1963, though Rosa Lewis had died in 1952.

Many of the old country inns which had survived the passing of the stage coach enjoyed a new lease of life in the late nineteenth century when cycling became all the rage, and the coming of the motor car enabled many of them to be rebuilt, often in the Tudor style. In the cities new hotels were built in the modernist style with chrome, streamlining, huge sand-blasted glass panels (made popular in ocean liners), mosaic floors, vivid colour, and vast open spaces. This was particularly true of American hotels, which set the tone. Many still exist in the original

Left: Air travel made Hong Kong into a tourist's Mecca, and hotels such as the Peninsula catered for the new breed of traveller, totally unlike those of an earlier age - businessmen, British colonial officials and their families, and perhaps the odd missionary

*Right: The Negresco
Hotel, Nice. With the
coming of the railroad,
air travel, Mediterranean
steamship cruises, and
the increasing ownership
of private yachts, the
southern coast of France
proved and still proves
irresistible.*

Art Deco style and are rightly regarded as masterpieces. Provincial hotels in Britain had became part of the Public House Trust Company in the early twentieth century, where there was an emphasis on good food, tea, coffee, and soft drink and although alcohol was naturally sold the managers did not get commission on it. By 1913 the company had 43 hotels and had acquired a nationwide reputation. Renamed Trust Houses, the company eventually became Trust Houses Forte, the largest chain in the UK (in 1938 it had 222 hotels), and one of the largest in the world.

Among the inter-war hotels were the Dorchester (1929) and the vast Cumberland Hotel at Marble Arch with 1000 bedrooms, all with private bathrooms. These lacked the intimacy and friendliness of the older hotels; the managers were administrators rather than hoteliers, and efficiency was valued above profitless hobnobbing with the guests. Hotels have been loved and venerated, the locations of novels and movies such as *Grand Hotel*, made in 1932 with Greta Garbo, and a disguised version of *Grand Hotel, Weekend at the Waldorf* (1945). Dozens of films were made with hotel backgrounds; it was the perfect formula – a set, slightly altered for each new film, would serve for half a dozen hotel films. During World War II when accommodation was hard to come by there was a plethora of film comedies of the no-room-at-the-inn genre.

In an age increasingly frenetic, the sedate slow-moving hotel scene seemed out of date. Quick service, lack of frills, ready access to telephones and later television, a loaded drinks cabinet and facilities in the room for making tea or coffee – these were what was wanted, not the toadyism of ancient waiters or the yawning gaps between courses in moth-eaten dining rooms. There was no time to be lost in unsigned endless corridors. Hotels were often seen as work-stations rather than as places to take one's ease. The romance was over.

INDEX

PICTURE CREDITS